Presentation by *BookLeaf Publishing*

Web: www.bookleafpub.com

E-mail: info@bookleafpub.com

ISBN: 9789358314465

First edition 2024

To Brian, my Brother in Christ

&

*To my Mom and Dad, without whom I am
incomplete*

ACKNOWLEDGEMENT

Thank You, Josh and Tina (Elm City Vineyard, New Haven), for Your prayers and the Artist Circle.

Thank You, Anna and Fisayo (Trinity Baptist Church, New Haven) for the Selah sessions!

&

Thank You, Sue and Karen (Rivendell Institute) for being so so motherly!

Holy are the Tears from your Eyes

Joseph cried. From the depths of the prison…Joseph cried.
For two years, no one came for him. Joseph cried.
How could the cup-bearer forget him so easily? Joseph cried.
Even sunlight forgot to enter his cell. Joseph cried.
Joseph cried. Joseph cried. Joseph cried.
The master he served so faithfully…never came for him. Joseph cried.
The brothers whom he loved…never came for him. Joseph cried.
His father, the faithful Jacob…could not come for him. Joseph cried.
Abandoned. Helpless. Exhausted. Defeated. Joseph cried.
So fell the salty tears on the rigid ground.
If You can see and hear him, God, won't You make a sound?
So You said, "Holy are you, Joseph, and Holy are the tears from your eyes.
I am Your God, Your Father, Your Light, and I accept your sacrifice.
I let you fall this far down, but now I'll make you rise,
So wipe your tears and rejoice, dear Joseph, for here comes your grand surprise!"

So make me Holy in Your eyes, God, when others don't come for
me,
I am not strong enough to break my own chains…or to set me free
-
When fires roar, I get burnt - my God, You don't!
When waters rise, I get drowned - my God, You don't!
When winds howl, I get scattered - my God, You don't!
When the hammer comes down, I shriek out - my God, You don't!
When time runs out, I panic - my God, You don't!
When it hurts, I cry out - my God, You don't!
So when I come home tired and helpless, left with no choice -
I just pray I do not miss the sound of Your voice.
Tell me then, "Holy are you, dear one, and Holy are the tears from
your eyes.
I am Your God, Your Father, Your Light, and I accept your
sacrifice.
I let you fall this far down, but now I'll make you rise,
So wipe your tears and rejoice, my dear one, for here comes your
grand surprise!"

(based on the story of Joseph, who was sold to slavery by his
brothers and punished unjustly by his master, but God made him
the second in command to the Pharaoh.)

Empty Nets

My nets are running empty Jesus, I have tried and tried and tried.
No fish I could catch anywhere, even my tears have gotten dried.
My nights have been quite exhausting, You know I have done my best,
I don't have any strength left in me...Lord, I need Your rest.

My empty nets look at me in ridicule, for fishing is all I know,
I know all the best fishing spots, where the cleverest fish can go.
I have been there now, and tried everything - all a man can do,
Giving up is not an option for me, but the emptiness is true.

So step into my boat, Lord Jesus, and tell me where to fish,
I am helpless without You, Lord Jesus,...Help me! - this I wish.
Help me catch the fish I need, Lord, beyond my wildest dreams,
May there be such an overflow that my nets break at the seams.

I pray this now with a broken heart; my mind is full of grief,
Give me hope and make me Yours, God, cure my unbelief!

(based on Luke 5 1:11 where Jesus helps his disciples catch more
fish than they can ever imagine after a long night of failures)

O! Mountain n' Vale

O! Mountain, get ready, for it's time for you to bow.
O! Valley, get ready, for it's your turn to rise.
Our God, slow to anger, has willed it now,
Each of you will receive your just prize.

Enough have you blocked the sun because you're tall,
Enough have you cast a shadow on our short days,
Enough have you said - you are mightier than us all.
O! Mountain, You've forgotten your God's ways.

God made you high to help others climb higher,
God gave you rivers and such a splendid peak,
Your people died because you sucked dry the river,
In your pride, you smashed them - those who are weak.

O! Valley, God has seen your ever-falling tears,
He knows deeply - how lonely you have been,
Since He is God, He has known your biggest fears,
The time is coming when He'll make you evergreen.

When you lay in the darkness, crying every night,
God was busy making plans - to cover you with light,
Plans to make you laugh again, plans to make you shine,
Stop crying, o my Vale!, you'll be more than just fine!

So praise our God, to Him we bow,
The maker of Hill and Vale,
For the valley would be a mountain now,
And the mountain would be vale.

(based on Isaiah 40:4,5 stating how God can change everything for
His glory and justice)

Through My Storms

Every time I slipped, You were there to hold me tight.
Every time I cried, You caught my tears.
Through the never-stopping hurricanes in my darkest night,
You called me to banish my fears.

Forgive me, my Lord, for I have failed You,
For I forgot - that You walk on the sea.
You silence all storms with a single rebuke,
'N even in this storm, You will not forsake me.

My heart leaped up when You asked me to be gallant,
My feet took flight, and I walked on the sea.
But the wind in the sails was too strong for my faith,
Even in Your presence, I screamed, "Save me! Save me!"

I am sure you chuckled at how stupid I am,
How easily I thought - I'm at the mercy of the waves.
How easily I forgot the miracles You have shown me,
How easily I forgot - it is the Son of God who saves.

You clasped my hand and pulled me up - how? I don't recall,
Was too numb to grasp Your hand, too scared to think at all.
I just know - You saved my life, when I froze in fear,
The waves chose not to harm me because You held me dear.

So, fill me up with Your strength, as I head into the night,
Dark clouds gather and new storms rise, 'tis now twilight.
My Lord and Savior, Christ, my Rock, assure me You are here,
In Your name, I will dream again - You are bigger than my fear.

I did not think this storm would ever die down,
I did not think the waves would be tame.
To the name of Jesus they all had to bow down,
There's always power in my Savior's name!

(based on the story of Peter in the Sea of Galilea)

My God is always Watching Over Me

My nostrils were snuffed with the smell of the wild,
With the heavy must of animals unbathed,
I stood there perplexed - Daniel, the exiled,
As I hoped to escape - this trap unscathed.

My ground shook as the sleeping lions rose,
Their gleaming eyes hungrily seeking a prey,
Lashing their tails, they drew rather close,
Ready to pounce on me without delay.

I could see the bones of the recent dead,
Their half-eaten carcasses starting to rot.
The increase in growls stirred up my dread,
I desperately sought a safe hiding spot.

But there was no place where I could hide,
I stood all alone in the lion's crowd,
Would anyone miss me, if here, I died?
The lions' roars were getting quite loud.

I could feel their foul breath upon my face,
I could hear the heavy claws scratching the stones.
"Show me Your mercy, show me Your grace,
O God, don't let them break my bones."

I have praised You through my times of laughter,
I have praised You through moments of doubt,
Please, please, please, God, - don't let me falter,
O God, You know - I have been devout.

So, Come O God, move Your hand,
And show Your power - this, I pray.
In Your mighty name, I take my stand,
From the impossible, please, make a way!

Wait! Are the same lions starting to walk back?
They are no longer hungry, but ready to sleep?
The once-roaring alpha retreating from attack,
The same pride of lions now, benign as sheep.

My eyes cannot believe what I am seeing,
My senses say - it all can't be true...
I thank You, my Lord, with all my being,
For nothing is impossible, unto You!

You silenced the lions of pride and boastfulness,
You silenced the lions of anxiety and despair,
You have silenced the lions of doubt and hopelessness,
You showed me again, how much You care.

The lions of fear, now lay fast asleep,
Their sharp claws of terror, laid to rest.
The lions of distress in slumber deep,
As I stand here saved, by Your grace.

Thank You, Lord, for having saved me,
For pulling me out from sure jaws of death.
Your powers in full display now, I see,
I will praise You till my dying breath.

I will not doubt You for the rest of the night,
But this I know - these lions will not stir,
I will walk by faith, and not just by sight,
I will spread Your glory here and far.

I don't know what plots, my enemies will start,
I don't know how happy, my king will be…
But this I know with all my heart -
My God is always watching over me.

(based on Daniel 6 where God protects Daniel in the den of lions)

Yoked

Why do You break me so many times God? To see my contrite heart?
I'm sorry I am blaming You, God - the fault was mine from the start.
You asked us to seek Your kingdom first, God - for You are just and fair,
Yet I fell for a person I liked, and thought - this was an answered prayer!
It's not that I didn't pray, O God, to You I did offer praise,
But my heart had found an idol, so I moved away from Your grace.

So it happened as You had foretold - my joy became my fears.
The pillows that held my head in peace once - now grew wet in tears.
My idol broke, my heart shattered, couldn't figure out what went wrong,
But through my shame and overwhelming numbness, You gave me back my song -
My song to declare my heart is Yours God, You will put it to kingdom use,
A broken and contrite heart, O God, You've said - You will not refuse.

You will find the one for me, God, I trust You through and through,
All I ask is - stay close to me, God, and keep me yoked to You!

(based on Psalm 51:17 stating God does not turn away a broken heart)

It's Time to Tell

Your morning may have seen darkness,
Your sun may have bled tears,
Clouds of pain may have chained you down,
O Israel! Come, let's fly above those fears!

It's time to tell - in Bethlehem - my savior has been born,
The chosen one to defeat death, when the veil will be torn.
He may lie in a manger - a helpless baby boy,
One day we'll be freed by Him, - and in Him, find joy.

It's time to tell - our God is faithful, His promises ever true,
He has come down to live with us,- and take home me and you,
He felt all alone in heaven - so He sent His only son,
He will wash us clean of all our sin,- and save us, everyone.

It's time to tell - I have a shepherd now, a savior always here,
Even through my valley of death, I can feel him - He is near.
I may be one in a million - the black sheep who is lost,
He will come and save me still, - for He has borne the cost.

In the Son of God and Prince of Peace, let all your hopes abound,
If you can lose yourself in Him, through Him, you will be found,
So smile, O Israel! The time is here - for all of us to tell -
Your Savior has been born tonight, and in Him, all is well.

(based on Luke 2 highlighting the birth of Jesus)

Let Your Will Be Done

May I open my lips tonight and sing to You, my Lord,
My words are lost in a distant haze…so pray for me, my God.
I do not know what I should ask - for glory or for grace,
So look into my heart, before You judge, not just at my face.

For I smile with a broken heart and a mask for everyone,
But no matter how far I fall, I know I am still Your son.
I have lost my wealth, I have lost my means, and You know that is true -
And none can pull me up from here - if You do not come through.

So I'm waiting Lord, I'm waiting, Lord, waiting for Your hand,
To end this pain once and for all, and part this quicksand.
My mind grows numb, and my fingers weak every passing day,
I am finally ready to do Your will…God, show me Your way.

You don't love me, I can't say that…for me, You gave Your only son,
Your plans are more grand than all I can think of…let Your will be done.

(based on Ephesians 5:15-18 where believers are asked to
surrender their plans to God's will)

Beloved!

My fingers could never grasp Your greatness, neither could my mind,
I thought I would never lose anyone - if I were warm and kind.
Sandstorms howl, cacti blossom, my beloved loses leaves,
My fingers latch on to my beloved's fingers - my mind silently grieves.
It's easy to count our blessings at birth, more difficult in times of death,
It's easy to find You in moments of triumph, difficult in tests of faith.

How strong are You my God - who can see His own son die,
I will never be that strong, my Lord, no matter how much I try!
So give me strength to walk this path, God; my beloved dies on Your vine,
Teach me how to hold unto You tight, and how to stop myself from crying,
Only Your promises can heal me now, God, the ones You made time and again,
That a believer would find their way to You, God, and Jesus didn't die in vain,
That Jesus would come to take us home one day - my fallen beloved and I,
Where there is no grief or pain - in Your castle in the sky!

(based on John 14:1-3 where Jesus promises to take all believers home to live with God)

How much He loves you all

When You took away my husband, there was nothing I could say.
My tears froze in my eyes, and my mind in dismay.
But I still had my little son, playing on the floor,
The one for whom, I have to strive, 'n live a little more.

I raised him honest, my little boy - into a man of trade,
But then one night, he fell ill, and he never left his bed.
The rabbi came, the doctors came, but it was all in vain,
After ten days of valiant fight, my son, too, died in pain.

So I lost everyone I had - everyone I held dear,
No reason left, for me to live on, how much can I bear?
As they took him to the deathbed to lay him in the ground,
I contemplated killing myself when no one would be around.
I prayed a lot, I prayed a lot, but my answers never came.
I thought I was God's mistake, and I was the one to blame.
I was ready to meet my maker now, once and for all -
"Take me back in Your arms, God, I am ready for Your call."

But You did not show up, God, instead You sent a man,
Who stopped our parade of mourning, and enacted Your plan.
He saw my tears, looked at me, and I forgot that I was sad,
The warmth in his eyes melted all the bitterness I have had.
He raised his hand and boldly said, "Young man, rise!"
And lo and behold! My dead son opened his two eyes!

I looked back at him, too bewildered to check - if this was true,
He smiled back with a look that said, "Daughter, I see you -
I was there when your husband died, I've seen your son fall.
Why do you think God will not come, even if you call?
I am placing you on the palm of my hand, where I will keep you warm,
Rain may come, hail may come, but I'll keep you through the storm.
You still have a lot to live for, so I am giving you back your son.
So praise the Spirit, praise the Father - the one and only One!
He does act tough sometimes, but so much He loves you all,
He is coming to stay in your hearts - the hearts of big and small.
So go and tell the good news now…in every village and town -
The Son of God is coming for you, and He will not let you down.
He will go before you in every battle, and never leave your side -
So love Him pure with all Your heart, and in Him, come abide!"

(based on Luke 7: 11-17 where Jesus was moved by the tears of a
widow losing her son and granted him back his life)

The One Who Stands for me

I have stood alone in courts of men. I have stood alone in a crowd.
I have stood alone in lots of pain, I have stood alone in doubt.
Then You came and told me that - You are bigger than my test,
All I need is to focus on You…And You will bring me rest.
You will catch me sad or angry or lost if I may be,
You will take over my every battle…You'll stand for me.

I didn't trust, I didn't believe, I thought You were a myth.
I read through Your books of glory but missed the truth beneath.
We live in a strange world indeed, where truth needs to be proved,
If enough men believe in a lie, truth, too, can be moved.
There are consequences for voicing truth; afraid we have to be -
If I am punished for the truth, who will stand for me?

Not everyone can be as strong as You, ready to be brave,
Defiant for the truth You stand for, truthful till the grave.
Flogged and whipped, jeered and mocked, skin peeled from bone,
Standing up for God's own truth, no one coming when You groan,
Peter denied, others ran, You should have chosen to be free,
Instead, You bore what I deserve…because You'll stand for me.

People didn't recognize You, the leaders got You wrong,
The entire crowd stood against You, yet You stood strong.
Pilate would have let You go - if only You gave in,

But You came to do His will, and to defeat sin.
You stood silent when they chose - Barabas to go free,
Men's truth would always fall, but You still stand for me.

They whipped you more, they shed more blood, they dragged You to the cross -
The king of all stood crucified, yet, He didn't count it as loss.
They thought that they had killed You off, and death will have its hold,
They didn't get who You really are, or would rise as God foretold.
So You tore the veil, and rose again, to sit on God's side of right,
Now I know why You can stand for me, and how we won the fight.

I am not as pure as You, Jesus, I deal in truth and lies,
Most of the decisions I take and live by - are nothing but unwise,
If God chooses to punish me every time, He will be in the right.
But You're the Son of God, the merciful, the One who yields all might.
So forgive me with Your divine power O Jesus, and build me up anew,
By Your truth, I stand rectified, and one who stands for me
is...You!

(based on John 18:28-19:42 where Jesus stands for God's truth and
is crucified to fulfill the prophecy - for the sake of all who believe
in Him)

Treasure

My brother had always kept us well, a man, godly and kind,
Yet he fell gravely ill one day, and no remedy could we find.
We sent word for Jesus, the healer - a man whom we called friend,
I wept and waited, wept and waited, he didn't turn up in the end.

Jesus showed up four days later, after my brother started to rot -
"If you believe, you'll see God's glory…did I tell you not?"
Saying this to me, Jesus now said, "Lazarus, come out!"
Praise be to God! My dead brother started moving about!

It was no witchcraft, it was no magic, it was a miracle pure,
Nothing was impossible for this man, for He IS the only cure!
I didn't know what to give to Him, for nothing He ever asks,
Only to trust in Him completely, and push aside other tasks.

So I brought forth the most expensive thing - a scent my brother
had got,
Some say it cost a whole year's wage - I guess it's worth a lot!
But to me, it was nothing at all; He raised up my brother from
dead,
I would have laid down my own life, if He had asked for that
instead.

I learned that day what real treasure means, and why true treasure
is love,
Why Jesus, who could have seized all power, stayed as gentle as a
dove.
If we get gold and silver coins, the wealth we try to store,
In the hope - when the time is right, we'll get things valued more.

But no matter, how much money we have, we cannot bribe death.
God does not seek gold or silver, but God does demand faith.
If Jesus had not seen my pitiful estate, and chosen to revive,
There's nothing on earth I could have given, that's worth my
brother's life.

He can't be bought; He can't be bullied, with Him, you can't strike
deals,
He would love you with His reckless love, and does only what God
wills.
He gave sight to the blind, hope to the poor and salvation to the
lost,
He fed the hungry, quelled the angry, but never mentioned cost.

Some loved Him for the miracles, and some for the gifts He
brought,
He knows who loves Him for the gifts, and who loves Him for
what He taught.
So, He often lets our hearts get broken, for that's when our hearts
are true -
All other treasures seem dull beside you, Jesus; my true treasure is
You!

(based on John 12:3 where Mary anoints Jesus for resurrecting her
brother)

The Fall of Two Thousand

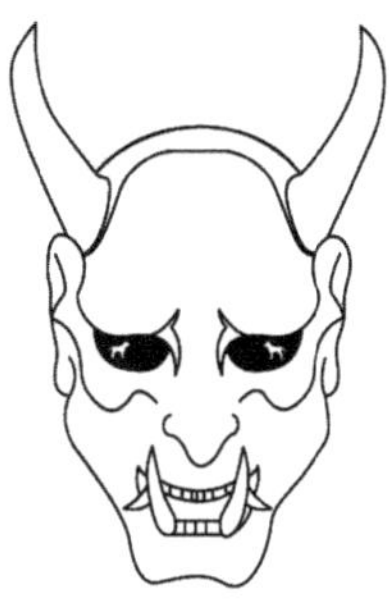

If you lose the gamble, he said, "All of yours would be mine."
I am pretty strong-willed, - so I thought, "All will be fine!"
Like a thief, they invaded my body for the gamble lost,
I never truly fathomed before - what a soul might cost.

But the one actually was a legion, and my soul got overthrown,
Two thousand they were, but I was all alone.
They kept me in the darkness and kept the light for their own,
Two thousand they were, but I was all alone.
They stole my life and family, so no one heard my groan,
For they were two thousand, but I was all alone.
From a man, I became a beast with my name no longer known,
For they were two thousand, but I was all alone.
They feasted on my body, and my pillow was a tombstone,
For they were two thousand, but I was all alone.

But then came my mighty Light, more radiant than the sun,
The Man to whom they surrendered, the King of everyone.
"Son of God, mighty Jesus, don't banish us from this region,
You are one, but We are many, the all-powerful Legion".
Jesus allowed for their wish to pass, so that I might go free,
Leaving me, they entered the pigs and drove them to the sea.
The herd started running off the cliff, screaming in howling pain,
As the last pig sank into the sea, I could move my body again!

(I said) "Take me with You, master! I will serve You every day".
(Jesus said) "But your job is different, so here, you have to stay -
Tell your story to everyone here, dressed shabbily or fine...
Of how the Legion fell to death, and with your Savior's light, you
shine!"

(based on Mark 5:1:20 the story of the demon-possessed man
whom Jesus saved)

You Won't Let me Down

I have lost my faith O Jesus, my faith like mustard seeds,
Where there was once a pretty garden, today it's full of weeds.
You say God's timing is perfect, but, I feel He's often late,
For some people, He is right on time, but that is not my fate.
Maybe He wants me to wait in patience, or maybe I'll need to act.
It takes courage and faith to receive His blessings - that is a true
fact!

Remember that unclean woman, O Jesus, the one who never
stopped bleeding?
The one forced to live, along the fringes, at our society's bidding?
The one whom You walked right past by, but she touched your
garment's helm,
When You felt the power leave You...You had asked her for her
name.
You said her faith had healed her, and it was a tale of courage too -
To be in a crowd that deeply hates her, and to reach out in faith to
You.

What would have happened if she didn't reach out? Or tried, but
she missed?
Or someone noticed and threw her out? Or grabbed her by the
wrist?
Would You have gone back to her, Jesus, for she was Yours to
heal?

Could You not have stopped for her, Jesus, if healing was your
Father's will?
But thank You, Jesus, for making her well - You were her only
hope,
For twelve years, she bled and bled, with no strength left to cope.

Everyone there had scolded her, Jesus, for she was out of place,
But Your love didn't see her estate; Your love had come from
grace.
You didn't judge her for the desperate act; Your healing set her
free,
If I am ever in that much pain, Jesus, promise You'll come for me.
I will not know whether to act or not, Jesus, or when to touch Your
gown,
I just know You will come for me, Jesus; You won't let me down!

(based on Mark 5:25-34 where the woman bleeding for twelve
years got healed by touching Jesus' robe)

Neither convenient nor easy

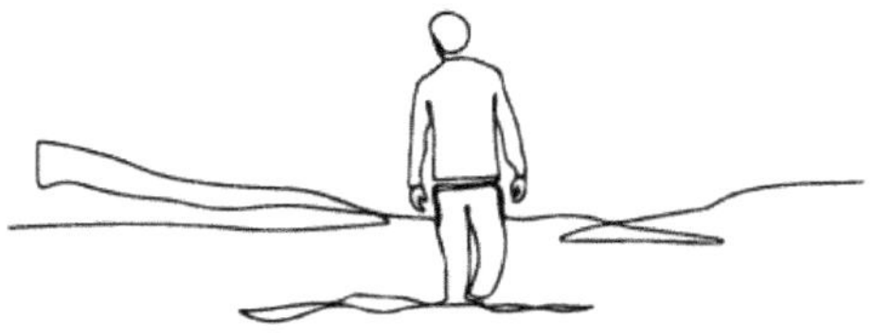

I am an ordinary man, I know ordinary trade.
I might be linked to King David, but he is long dead.
He had commanded legions, but I command none.
Is putting me through all these tests, Your idea of fun?

I am not ungrateful, God, for You've blessed me 'n my life,
As any man would have, I sought purity in my wife.
But then I came to know one day, that she's already with child,
Why would You do that, Lord? Give me a woman defiled?

I may not be the King of twelve tribes, but I have followed Your
laws,
Why are You penalizing me so harshly, for my simple flaws?
I will divorce Mary silently, so that, others don't come to know,
"Tell me Father, what I should do now? Or to whom I should go!"

Your angel came and said, "O Joseph, son of David, the King,
This child is from the Holy Spirit, and the light that He will bring
Will save the fallen sons of Adam, and the lost daughters of Eve.
This child will be God's best miracle yet; this You must believe".

Who am I to argue with You, Lord? I did as You had told,
And Your son stepped into this Earth, on a night cold.
In the manger, amidst the sheep, He was born in Bethlehem,
As You had commanded us before, - we gave Him the Jesus name.

Your plan does not make sense at all, You send three men from afar
To gift the baby boy with lots of gold, frankincense, and myrrh.
Yet, You do not grant this boy - a midwife or a bed,
He was born like a destitute - where cows and goats are fed.

You have asked us to bow down to You - to Your perfect will.
My heart breaks for this little child, helpless I do feel.
He is not my flesh and blood, and yet, I hold Him dear,
When Herod tried to hunt Him down, for Him, I did fear.

When our King Herod died, - I felt a lot of bliss,
Your angel came and told me now,- "Go to Israel in peace".
But Herod's son was now in Judea; from there, he would reign,
And Your precious child will be in...danger once again!

So I am taking Him to Nazareth, where no one ever goes,
This sacrifice I will have to make, to protect Him from foes.
When they sing of David's tales, the stories of his rise,
I don't think they will remember me, or my sacrifice.

I am sure You are writing a grander story - one I cannot see,
But I admit the journey has neither been convenient nor easy.
For the ways, You have protected the child, thank You, I must,
An ordinary me bows to an extraordinary God, and in You, I trust!

(based on Matthew 1 and 2 - specifically Matthew 2:19-23 where
Joseph took shelter in Nazareth with Mary and baby Jesus)

Multiplied

Five loaves of bread and two fish.
In the hands of Jesus, they multiplied.

He thanked God, and they multiplied.
Thousands ate. Yet they multiplied.
In the hands of Jesus, they multiplied.

It was everyday bread. Yet they multiplied.
It was very common fish. Yet they multiplied.
Carried by a nameless boy. Yet they multiplied.
In the hands of Jesus, they multiplied.

Five thousand were hungry. Yet they multiplied.
Five thousand were sated. Yet they multiplied.
His disciples were helpless. Yet they multiplied.
His disciples were elated. Yet they multiplied.
In the hands of Jesus, they multiplied.

It was not about the food. So they multiplied.
It was not about who ate. So they multiplied.
It was not about the when. So they multiplied.
In the hands of Jesus, they multiplied.

He trusted God. So they multiplied.
They trusted Him. So they multiplied.
In the hands of Jesus, they multiplied.

Don't have much today? It's okay! Bring them to Him. Trust. Pray.
In the end, You will say - in the hands of Jesus, they multiplied.

(based on Matthew 14:13-21 where Jesus fed the five thousand)

Glasshouses and Stones

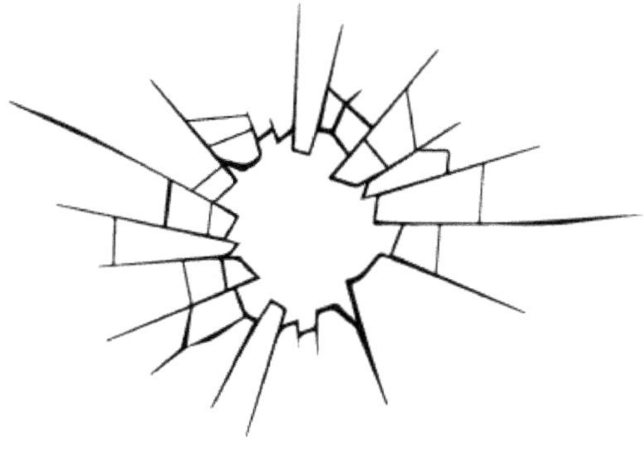

Are we not all like glasshouses?
Waiting for people to see -
The wonderful colors we hold inside.
Waiting for people to say -
We hold wonderful colors inside.

What happens if they don't?
Instead, they see a vortex of black and gray
And it scares them.
Or, they see an exotic blend of gold and silver
And it still scares them.

What if we are all scared?
Scared if our colors don't match,
That might make us weak.
Or scared if our colors do match,
That might make us weak.

Or we are not scared at all!
To start throwing stones at those -
Whose colors are different!
Or start throwing stones at those -
Who won't change colors to match our own!

We love our stones.
There's something easy about loose stones.
Very easy to pick. Very easy to kick.
Ultra-light on our fingers.
Easy to point. Easy to throw.

Stones hurtling through the air.
Hitting the glass. Smashing it.
The colors come gushing out.
More stones. More colors spouting out.
Throwing stones is fun.

We love our stones.
We love throwing them together.
We cheer when the glass shatters.
We find more stones to throw together.
The more the glass breaks, the more stones we throw.

We just forget someone else can throw a stone at us, too!
That there is someone whom a crowd cannot scare.
That there is someone who sees through opaque walls.
That there is someone who sees our true colors.
That there is someone mightier yet more merciful.

One time, some "sinless" men were about to stone a sinful woman.
Her red was about to spout out. The crowd was ready to cheer.
A man in white shielded her. He wrote something on the ground.
And asked the "sinless" to cast the first stone. The crowd left.
Not a single stone got thrown that day. So the woman lived.

Years later, some "sinless" men threw stones at the man in white.
His red came gushing out. They shattered His glass walls.
Yet, He said - forgive the ones who throw the stones.
There is indeed someone mightier yet more merciful.
So He rose from the dead. Again, in white. Smiling.

I still throw stones from time to time.
But He does not. He can. He does not.
Sometimes, I feel sad and mad. I cannot control it.
I am trying hard not to throw stones anymore.

I am sorry. What about you?

(based on John 8:1-11 where Jesus protected a woman from getting
stoned to death)

Shout Out

I have been pushed over. I have been kicked.
What others threw out, is what I have picked.
No one really wants me, they tend to ignore,
Unless I am begging in front of their door.

They all tend to boot me; some let me stay,
As long as I promise, I won't come back next day.
I am mostly invisible; I'm lost in the noise,
Everyone tries to ignore a blind beggar's voice.

"Silence!" they rebuked, when I shouted Your name,
A lowly beggar is always easier to blame.
After receiving years of indifference 'n abuse,
I shouted louder, for I had nothing to lose.

"Son of David, Son of David, have mercy on me!
Rabbi, Rabbi, O great Jesus, I want to see."
You asked me to come closer, and in Your voice kind,
(Said) "Your faith has healed you. You are no longer blind!"

Your words put an end to my longsuffering night,
My darkness dissolved into the new day's sunlight.
Had I not shouted loud or had lost my faith,
I would remain without sight till my very death.

So if others try to stifle you, don't stop, just shout -
In the name of Jesus Christ, without any doubt!
He will surely stop by, for He knows you're in pain,
Sometimes He takes a while...so, don't stop, shout again!

(based on Mark 10:46-52 where Jesus heals the blind beggar
Bartimaeus)

www.ingramcontent.com/pod-product-compliance
Lightning Source LLC
LaVergne TN
LVHW010834200726
843508LV00012B/2606